Photo credits

Bryan Alexander 35 below; All Sport 45 below; Aspect Picture Library 46-47; Heather Angel/Biofotos 11 below right, 16, 23 above right, 24 below; Ron Boardman 39 above; J Allan Cash 6, 33 above; Bruce Coleman 35 above, 42; Douglas Dickins 28,28-29,33 below; French Government Tourist Office 39 above; Geoslides 34-35; Robert Harding Associates 29 below, 44 above; Hughes Aircraft Company 21; Alan Hutchison Library 2-3, 4-5, 23 above left, 25 below, 26-27 below, 29 above, 38 below, 48 below; London Stone 43 above and below; Stella Martin 23 below, 30-31 below, 36 below; Meteorological Office (Crown copyright) 20-21; Museum of London 39 below; National Hurricane Center 20, 21 above; Natural Science Photos 7, 24 above, 25 above; R.K. Pilsbury 11 above, 14 above, 15 above and below, 16-17; G.R. Roberts 9; Science Photo Library 18; ZEFA 8, 10-11, 11 below left, 14 below, 22 above and below, 24-25, 26-27 above, 27, 30-31 above, 31 above and below, 32-33 above and below, 34, 36 above, 42-43, 44 below, 45 above.

First published in Great Britain in 1983 by
Macmillan Publishers Limited

This edition published in 1990 by
Treasure Press
Michelin House
81 Fulham Road
London SW3 6RB

© Macmillan Publishers Limited

ISBN 1 85051 405 4

Printed in Portugal

·THE · CHILDREN'S · ILLUSTRATED · LIBRARY·

WEATHER AND CLIMATE

Keith Lye

TREASURE PRESS

Contents

Dark clouds approach Hong Kong from the sea. Some severe storms that hit Hong Kong are typhoons. This is the term used for hurricanes in the China Sea. These storms bring intense rain and strong winds.

Observing the Weather

'Red sky at night, shepherds' delight. Red sky at morning, shepherds' warning.' This is one of many old sayings about the weather. Such sayings were used to help people predict the weather long before radio and television stations began to issue weather forecasts every few hours.

People have always been interested in the weather. We all want to know whether we should take a raincoat with us when we go out, or whether our favourite sport will be held up by bad weather. Air pilots, ships' captains and even motorists need to know about weather conditions so that they can travel safely. Farmers, perhaps more than any other people, are at the mercy of the weather – an unexpected frost or hailstorm can destroy their crops. In some parts of the world, too much rain can cause destructive floods, while in the following year a drought may cause widespread starvation.

What is Weather?

Weather is the condition of the air at a certain time or over a brief period of time. The term includes the temperature and pressure of the air, winds and how much moisture the air contains. These and other factors combine to give us fine, sunny days or cold, wet ones. The study of weather is called meteorology. Meteorologists study the atmosphere, the thin envelope of air around the Earth, and the causes of weather. Some work at weather stations, collecting information, while others work at forecasting centres.

Climate and Weather

Climate differs from weather, because climate is the average or usual weather of a place. Climatologists study climate and how it affects people, plants and animals. They are interested in past climatic changes and in whether climates will change in the future. They also want to find out in what way human activities may alter climates.

Ethiopia, in north-eastern Africa, has cool, rainy uplands and hot, dry lowlands, where droughts often occur. Here, Galla people collect water which has been brought into the drought-stricken area by lorry.

Without the atmosphere, life on Earth would not exist. It contains oxygen, which we breathe. Oxygen makes up 20.95 per cent of the air. Nitrogen makes up 78.09 per cent, argon 0.93 per cent, and other gases, including carbon dioxide, which plants need, 0.03 per cent. In the upper atmosphere there is a thin layer of gas called ozone, which filters out most of the Sun's harmful ultraviolet rays. The atmosphere is like a greenhouse. It lets sunlight (solar radiation) reach the surface, but it absorbs heat radiated from the surface, stopping all of it from escaping into space.

Although invisible, the atmosphere has weight. This can be proved by a laboratory experiment. First, pump the air out of a bottle and seal and weigh it. Then let air into the bottle again. It will now weigh more. Very roughly, the air in a drinking-glass weighs about the same as an aspirin tablet. The whole atmosphere weighs about 5,000 million million tonnes. In fact, about one kilogram of air is always pushing in on every square centimetre of our bodies; but there is an equal pressure inside our bodies.

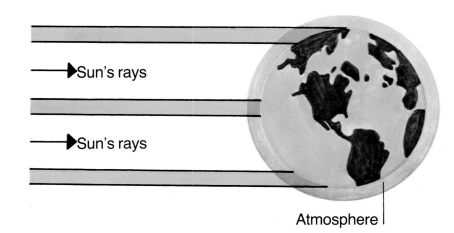

Atmosphere

All life on Earth depends on heat from the Sun. The amount of heat that reaches the Earth's surface varies from place to place. Generally the Sun's heat is greatest around the Equator, but it diminishes towards the poles. The atmosphere (the belt of air around the Earth) absorbs some of the Sun's heat. Because the Sun's rays have to pass through a greater thickness of atmosphere near the poles, more heat fails to reach the ground than at the Equator. The Sun's rays are also spread over a larger area and so are less effective near the poles.

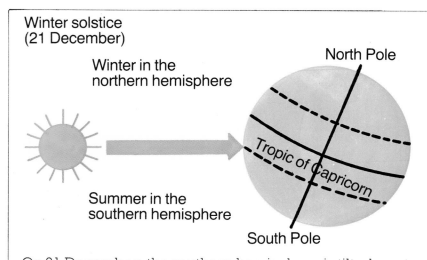

On 21 December, the southern hemisphere is tilted most towards the Sun, which is overhead at the Tropic of Capricorn (latitude 23½ degrees South). 21 December is the Winter Solstice in the northern hemisphere, but it is the Summer Solstice in the southern.

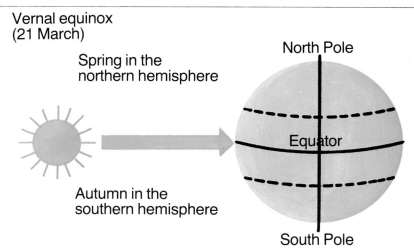

On 21 March, the Sun is overhead at the Equator. The Sun's rays are evenly spread over the Earth and all places on Earth have equal day and night, 12 hours each. 21 March is the Vernal (Spring) Equinox in the northern hemisphere and the Autumn Equinox in the southern.

The atmosphere is divided into four main layers. About 80 per cent of all the air in the atmosphere is in the lowest layer, the troposphere. This layer is about 18 kilometres thick over the Equator and 8 kilometres thick over the poles. Most weather conditions occur in the troposphere. Above the troposphere is the stratosphere, which extends up to 80 kilometres above the surface. The stratosphere contains most of the rest of the air in the atmosphere and the important ozone layer. The air there is much thinner. Above the stratosphere is the rarefied ionosphere, between 80 and 500 kilometres above the surface. Beyond, the exosphere merges into space.

Because the air gets thinner, the air pressure gets lower as one travels up into the atmosphere. Air pressure also varies on the ground. The Sun warms the surface and the surface heats the air. When air is heated, it expands and becomes lighter. Because warm air is lighter (or less dense) than cold air, it tends to rise, while cold air tends to sink. Rising warm air has a lower pressure than sinking cold air.

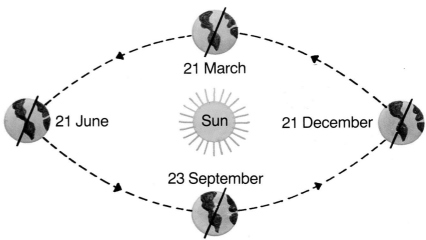

The Earth's axis, an imaginary line joining the North and South poles, is tilted by 23½ degrees. This means that, as the Earth travels around the Sun, the northern and southern hemispheres are sometimes tilted towards and sometimes away from the Sun. The northern hemisphere is tilted most towards the Sun on 21 June. As a result, it gets more sunlight than the southern hemisphere. But, on 21 December, it is tilted away from the Sun and so the southern hemisphere gets more sunlight than the northern. On 21 March and 23 September, the hemispheres share the sunlight evenly.

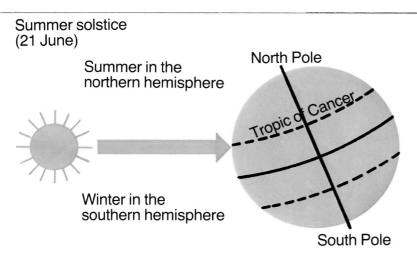

Summer solstice (21 June)

On 21 June, the northern hemisphere is tilted most towards the Sun, which is overhead at the Tropic of Cancer (latitude 23½ degrees North). 21 June is the Summer Solstice in the northern hemisphere and the Winter Solstice in the southern hemisphere.

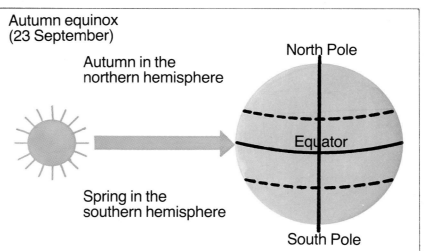

Autumn equinox (23 September)

On 23 September, the Sun is again overhead at the Equator. This is the Autumn Equinox in the northern hemisphere and the Vernal (Spring) Equinox in the southern. The word *Equinox* means 'equal night', because the lengths of the night and day are equal.

Temperature is the most important factor affecting weather. The Sun's heat is most intense at the Equator, where it is concentrated over a much smaller area than at the poles. The Earth's axis is tilted by 23½ degrees and, as a result, the amount of heat received at any place varies according to the time of the year. On 21 March and September 23, when the Earth is sideways on to the Sun, the Sun is overhead at the Equator. On these days – the equinoxes – the Sun's heat is shared equally by the two hemispheres. But at the solstices, 21 June and 21 December, first the northern and then the southern hemispheres lean towards the Sun, with one hemisphere getting more sunlight and heat than the other. This explains why we have seasons.

Left: The hot deserts of the world have only two seasons: winter and summer. Summer is the hottest season, and winter is cooler. This desert is in Libya, in North Africa. The world's highest shade temperature, 58°C, was recorded at Al-Aziziyah in Libya.

Sabah, part of Malaysia in north-eastern Borneo, has an equatorial climate. It is hot and rainy all the year round. There are no marked seasons in such areas. The trees in the dense forests grow throughout the year. They grow to great heights in order to reach the sunlight.

The Moving Air

The atmosphere is always moving because of the Sun's heat. Currents of air across the Earth's surface are what we call winds. There are also strong air currents above the surface. For instance, at the Equator, hot air rises rapidly above the low air pressure zone, the doldrums. The warm air gradually cools and spreads out north and south. It sinks down around the high air pressure horse latitudes, from which trade winds blow towards the doldrums and westerly winds blow towards the poles.

Trade winds, westerlies and polar easterlies (cold, dense winds from the poles) are the world's prevailing winds. These winds do not blow north-south, but are deflected by the Coriolis effect, caused by the Earth's rotation on its axis. So the trade winds north of the Equator blow from the north-east to the south-west.

Other factors, such as mountain ranges or friction with the land, affect winds. And in high and low pressure air systems (anticyclone and depressions), winds spiral around the centre, like bath water around an open plug-hole. Monsoon winds change direction according to the season (*see page 28*).

Wind speeds are classified on the Beaufort scale. On this scale of 0 to 12, 0 represents calm air, 8 is a gale with wind speeds of 63-74 kilometres per hour, and 12 is a hurricane (over 116 kilometres per hour).

Below: Although air is invisible, the sight of waves lashing the shore and clouds scurrying across the sky remind us that the atmosphere is always on the move. The clouds consist of a mass of tiny droplets of water and ice crystals. They may bring rain, snow or sleet.

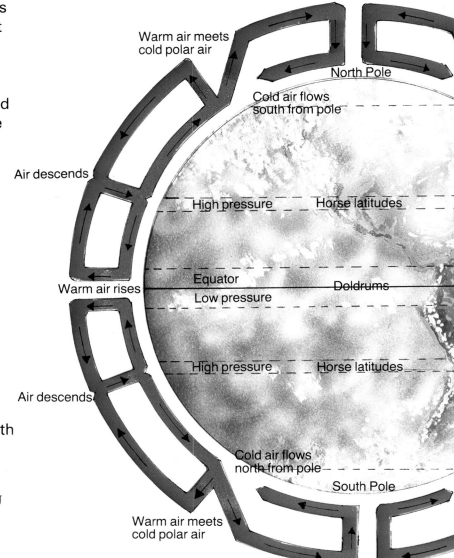

Warm air meets cold polar air

North Pole

Cold air flows south from pole

Air descends

High pressure — Horse latitudes

Warm air rises — Equator — Doldrums
Low pressure

High pressure — Horse latitudes

Air descends

Cold air flows north from pole

South Pole

Warm air meets cold polar air

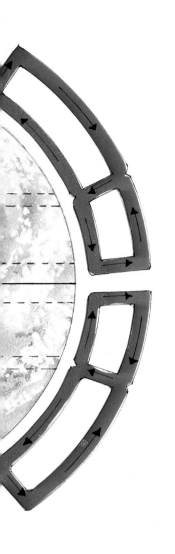

Left: At the Equator, the land is heated as hot air rises upwards. Hot air is lighter, or less dense than cold air, and so the air pressure around the Equator, a zone called the doldrums, is low. The hot air cools as it rises and eventually flows to the north and south. It sinks back to the Earth around the horse latitudes – zones of high air pressure. From the horse latitudes, some air flows back towards the Equator and some towards the poles.

Above: Winds are currents of air which we can feel, but not see. However, we can see the effects of winds, for example when they rustle the leaves of trees. Strong winds that nearly always blow from the same direction are called prevailing winds. In exposed areas, such winds can prevent trees from growing upright. Instead, the winds push saplings over so that the fully-grown trees are bent over in the direction of the prevailing wind.

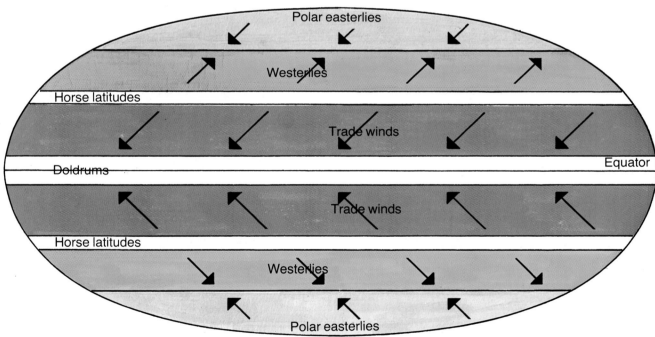

The map shows that prevailing winds generally blow over the surface from areas of high air pressure towards areas of low air pressure. For example, the north-east trade winds blow from the horse latitudes (around latitude 30 degrees North) towards the doldrums, the zone of low air pressure around the Equator. In the southern hemisphere, the south-east trade winds blow from the horse latitudes (around latitude 30 degrees South) towards the doldrums.

Westerly winds are other prevailing winds. They blow from the horse latitudes towards the poles. These warm winds eventually meet up with cold, dense air currents flowing from the poles. These air currents are winds called polar easterlies. Winds are deflected by the Earth's rotation.

All air contains water vapour, an invisible gas. Nearly all of this vapour is in the troposphere. Water vapour is continuously formed as the Sun evaporates the sea and lakes, and plants give off water vapour. The temperature determines how much water vapour the air can hold. Warm air can hold much more water vapour than cold air. So, the air over hot deserts often contains much more vapour than the air over cool temperate lands. But the water vapour in the hot air seldom condenses into visible water droplets, because condensation occurs only when the air cools below dew point.

Dew point is the temperature at which the air is saturated with moisture. Meteorologists say that the air at dew point has a relative humidity of 100 per cent. The relative humidity is the ratio between the actual amount of water vapour in the air and the maximum amount that it could hold at that temperature.

Meteorologists measure relative humidity with instruments called hygrometers. One of these instruments consists of two thermometers. One, the dry bulb thermometer, measures the actual air temperature. The other, a wet bulb thermometer, has a piece of wet muslin wrapped around its bulb. This muslin is dipped in a bowl of water so that it stays wet. The lower the humidity, the greater is the rate of evaporation from the muslin. Evaporation of water has a cooling effect. It makes the temperature of the wet bulb thermometer fall. The relative humidity is worked out from the difference in the temperatures on the two thermometers. There is a drawing of this instrument on page 19. Absolute humidity is a measurement of the actual amount of water vapour in the air.

Below dew point, water vapour in the atmosphere condenses around tiny bits of dust, soil or salt from the oceans to form visible drops of water or ice crystals. These particles are so small that they remain suspended in the air. Masses of these particles form clouds in the air, and fog, mist, frost and dew near the ground. In some clouds, water droplets are 'super-cooled'. This means that their temperature is below freezing point, but the water droplets are still in a liquid state.

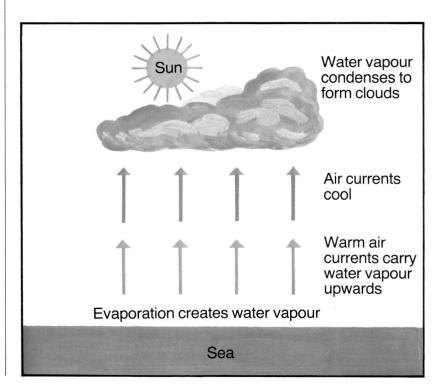

Above: Fog and mist are clouds at ground level. They often collect in valleys and tall buildings, such as church spires, may project through them. They form on calm, clear nights. Water vapour in the cooling air condenses into water droplets. These droplets are so light that they are suspended in the air and do not fall to the ground like heavy raindrops.

In a mist, we can see more than 1,000 metres, but less than 2,000 metres. Fogs are thicker. In fogs, the visibility is less than 1,000 yards and it may drop to only a metre or so. Mist and fog clear when temperatures rise.

Left: All air contains an invisible gas called water vapour. Over seas and lakes, the Sun's heat evaporates water which becomes water vapour. The water vapour is swept upwards as the warm air rises in strong currents. As the air rises, it gradually cools. Cold air cannot hold as much water vapour as warm air. Hence, the water vapour finally condenses around tiny specks of dust, salt, or other matter in the air. It forms minute water droplets, or sometimes ice crystals. Masses of these droplets or crystals form clouds high above the Earth's surface.

Above: The ice crystals sparkling on the tree are a kind of frost called rime. Rime forms when super-cooled water droplets (droplets that have a temperature below freezing-point but are still liquid) instantly freeze when they come into contact with objects.

Another kind of frost is glazed frost. It consists of coatings of smooth ice. It forms when rain falls on cold surfaces and freezes. Glazed frost sometimes coats telegraph and telephone wires, and becomes so heavy that it may bring the wires down. Hoar frost on windowpanes consists of patterns of ice crystals. These are formed from dew or from water vapour that condenses directly to become ice.

We can watch condensation taking place in a kitchen where the warm air contains a lot of invisible water vapour. Much of this water vapour is formed when water is evaporated from boiling saucepans and kettles. When the warm air comes into contact with a cold windowpane, the water vapour condenses into large droplets of water.

Dew is moisture deposited on cobwebs, blades of grass or other objects. The moisture is formed from water vapour which condenses on to the objects when the air is cooled below dew point. Dew point is the temperature at which the air is saturated – that is, the air contains all the water vapour that it can at that temperature.

Animals and plants on the land need a regular supply of fresh water. This comes from the salty oceans through the water cycle. The oceans contain about 97 per cent of the world's water. Over the oceans, the Sun's rays evaporate water which becomes water vapour. Rising air currents carry this water vapour upwards. As the air rises, it gradually cools. It finally passes dew point, when the water vapour condenses into clouds.

Winds blow the clouds over land areas. The winds are often forced to rise over ranges of hills and mountains. This causes further cooling. The clouds grow larger until the moisture in the clouds falls to the ground as precipitation. This may take the form of rain, snow, sleet or hail.

The main kind of precipitation in temperate regions is rain. Some of the rain sinks into the soil and is absorbed by the roots of plants. Some of the moisture used by plants soon returns to the air through transpiration. Transpiration means the giving off of water vapour by plant leaves. Some water sinks

through the soil into the rocks below. Water can seep through some rocks, such as sandstone, which contains many tiny pores, and limestone, which contains many cracks, passages and cave networks. Water seeping through rocks is called ground water. Ground water may return to the surface in springs, the sources of rivers. But it may flow all the way back to the sea without ever surfacing again. Some rainwater does not sink into the soil. Instead, it runs over the surface into rivers. Rivers then carry the water back to the sea,

again completing the water cycle.

In mountain and polar regions, the chief form of precipitation is snow. Snow often piles up and becomes compressed into ice. Large bodies of ice, ranging from huge ice sheets to valley glaciers, flow downhill towards the sea. On coasts, icebergs break away from ice sheets and glaciers. the icebergs melt in the sea, so completing the water cycle in another way. The water cycle may be interrupted, such as when people build dams across rivers.

Clouds are formed by the condensation of water vapour well above ground level. There are two main types: cumuliform, or heap, clouds; and stratiform, or layer, clouds. Cumuliform clouds have great depth. They are formed by strong upward air currents and they have a high moisture content. Stratiform clouds form in thin layers when moist air is slowly uplifted. Clouds are clues to future weather conditions.

Low clouds form within 2,500 metres of the ground. They include *stratus,* a grey layer cloud that is like a fog in mid-air. Stratus cloud often blocks out the Sun, although weak sunlight may be seen in thinner patches. Stratus clouds are associated with the warm fronts of depressions (*see page 17*) and they bring rain in summer and snow in winter. *Cumulus* is a white, heap cloud. It resembles large balls of cotton-wool. Fair-weather, fluffy cumulus cloud is seen in summer. But cumulus cloud may grow into huge *cumulonimbus* cloud. Cumulonimbus cloud is a dark and heavy cloud that may be 4,500 metres or more high between its often ragged base and its frequently anvil-shaped top. Cumulonimbus cloud is associated with thunder, lightning, hail, sleet and rain.

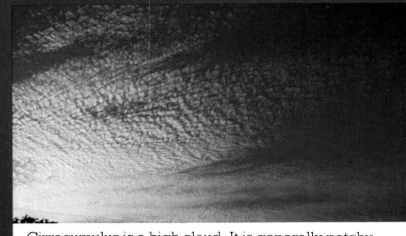
Cirrocumulus is a high cloud. It is generally patchy and composed of ripples or rounded masses.

Cumulus is a fluffy heap cloud. It forms within about 2,500 metres of the ground.

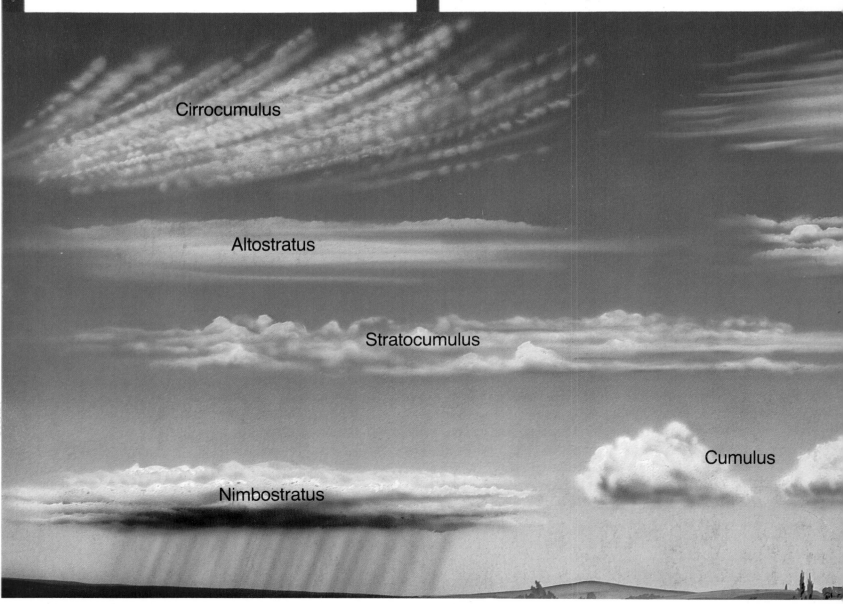
Cirrocumulus

Altostratus

Stratocumulus

Cumulus

Nimbostratus

Another low cloud is *nimbostratus.* This dark grey cloud is also associated with rain and snow. But the rain is not usually as heavy as that from cumulonimbus cloud, although it is often more prolonged. The fifth low cloud, the greyish-white *stratocumulus* cloud, consists of rounded masses or rolls that are so close together that they join up.

There are two kinds of medium cloud between 2,500 and 6,100 metres. *Altocumulus* cloud looks like a mass of little clouds. It is a sign of unsettled weather. *Altostratus* cloud is greyish or bluish in colour. It sometimes forms in thin layers, but it may be so thick that it blocks out the Sun. It often appears as a depression approaches.

High clouds form above 6,100 metres. They include *cirrocumulus* cloud, which consists of small balls of white cloud interspersed with tiny clear patches. Formed from ice crystals, cirrocumulus cloud is often called mackerel sky. *Cirrostratus* cloud is a soft, milky layer formed from ice and showing ripples and rounded masses. *Cirrus* cloud is delicate and feathery. It is often called mares' tails or ice banners. Farmers work especially hard when they see cirrus cloud approaching, because it is the first sign of an advancing depression.

Cirrus is a wispy, delicate cloud that forms from ice crystals at high levels in the atmosphere.

Lightning is caused by huge electrical sparks in clouds that light up the sky.

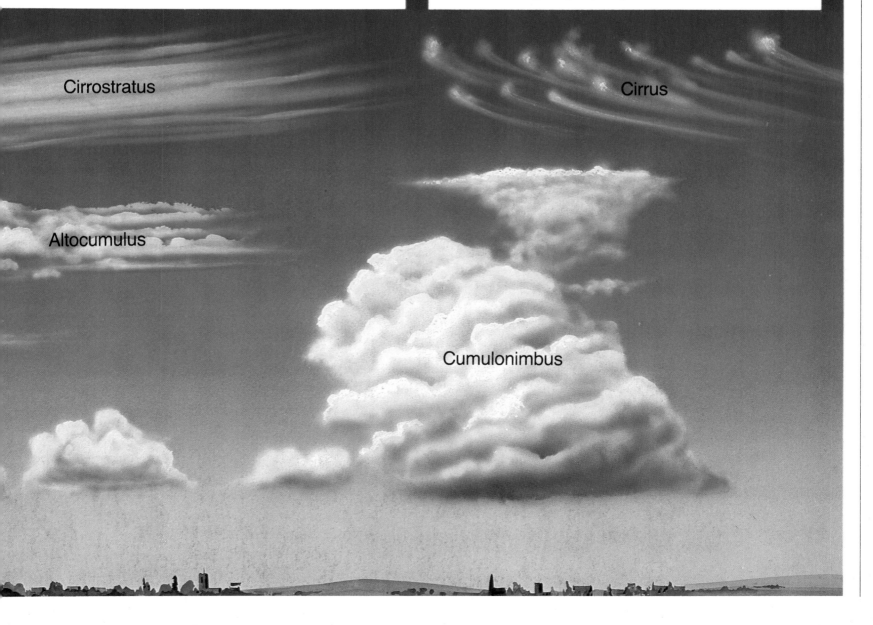
Cirrostratus

Cirrus

Altocumulus

Cumulonimbus

One feature of the weather that concerns everyone is rain. Rain forms in two main ways. In tropical regions, clouds are composed of millions of water droplets. As the warm air rises rapidly, the water droplets floating in the air collide with each other. As they collide, they fuse together into larger and larger drops. Finally, they are large enough to fall as raindrops through the rising air. Some raindrops never reach the ground. They evaporate in warm air beneath the cloud. This explains why the bottoms of some clouds are dark and ragged, although no rain reaches the ground.

In temperate regions, the tops of clouds are often below freezing point. Such clouds consist of tiny ice crystals and many more super-cooled water droplets. These water droplets, whose temperature is below freezing point, instantly turn into ice when they collide with an ice crystal. In the turbulent air, the ice crystals grow rapidly in size. Finally, they fall, usually passing through warmer air. They then melt to become raindrops.

Understanding of this process has enabled scientists to make rain fall. They do this by flying above a cloud and 'seeding' it with ice crystals, or the crystals of other substances, such as silver iodide. The silver iodide crystals are very similar to ice crystals and they grow in size when they collide with super-cooled water droplets. But successful rain-making is hard to achieve.

Above: Quickly growing cumulus clouds are being formed offshore by rapidly rising air currents. These currents are sweeping water vapour evaporated from the ocean into the air, where it condenses. When the clouds reach the land, they will probably bring heavy showers. If there are mountains near the coast, the winds are forced to rise. The air is chilled and the clouds grow in size. Heavy rain then falls on the mountain slopes. For example, the forested mountain ranges of western North America receive heavy rainfall from winds from the Pacific Ocean.

Left: In winter, snow often falls on mountain areas, instead of rain. Snow blankets the Scottish Cairngorm Mountains, left, and the reindeer have to hunt for food under the snow.

Right: Convectional rain occurs in warm regions. The top diagram shows that intense heating of the land evaporates moisture. Strong upward air currents make the air cool and cumulus clouds start to form. These clouds grow rapidly in size to become towering cumulonimbus, or thunder clouds. In some equatorial regions, especially near lakes, convectional rain falls nearly every day in the late afternoon.

The second diagram shows the formation of another kind of rain, called orographic rain. This occurs when warm winds from the sea are cooled as they rise over mountain ranges. As they rise, the air cools and clouds form. The clouds grow in size until rain or snow falls. On the far, or leeward, side of the mountains, the winds blow downhill. They get warmer as they descend and evaporate moisture from the land. Areas on the leeward sides of mountains are often arid. They are said to be rain shadow areas.

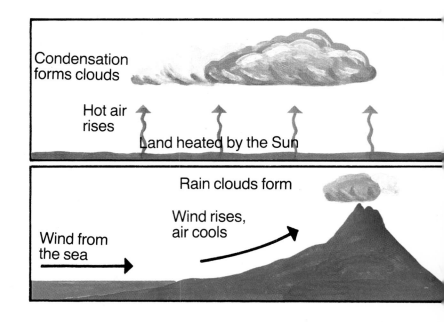

Condensation forms clouds

Hot air rises

Land heated by the Sun

Rain clouds form

Wind rises, air cools

Wind from the sea

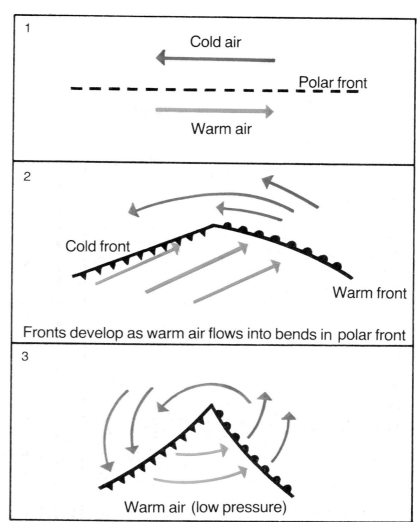

1

Cold air → Polar front

Warm air →

2

Cold front   Warm front

Fronts develop as warm air flows into bends in polar front

3

Warm air (low pressure)

When ice crystals fall from clouds in winter, they may pass through cold air. Such crystals do not melt, but become snowflakes. Sleet is a mixture of snow and rain. Hailstones often form in cumulonimbus clouds.

Cumulonimbus clouds form in warm places when intense heating of the land causes evaporation and convection currents in the air. Rain formed in this way is called convectional rain. Orographic rain occurs when warm air is cooled as it flows over mountains, while cyclonic rain occurs in cyclones, or depressions.

Depressions are low air pressure systems, often called 'lows'. In depressions in the northern hemisphere, winds rotate in an anticlockwise direction, while the opposite applies in the southern hemisphere. Depressions form along the polar front (see diagram). The light, warm air in depressions does not mix easily with the cold, dense air. Instead, beyond the warm front (the front edge of the warm air on the ground), warm air flows slowly upwards over the cold air. Clouds, mostly of the layer type, are formed.

Along the cold front, the cold air pushes under the warm air like a wedge. This makes the warm air rise steeply. As a result, cumulonimbus clouds may form behind the cold front. Eventually, the cold front closes up on the warm front, lifting the warm air completely above the ground. This is called an occlusion. Along occlusions, cloud and rain persist for some time until the depression dies out.

Depressions cause unsettled weather in many parts of the middle latitudes. The other main air system in these latitudes is the anticyclone. These are regions of high air pressure. Winds rotate around these systems in a clockwise direction in the northern hemisphere and in an anticlockwise direction in the southern hemisphere. Anticyclones are associated with settled weather. In summer, there may be a succession of hot, sunny days. But in winter, anticyclones may bring cold weather and fogs.

Above: The diagrams show the formation of depressions, which are also called cyclones or lows. These low pressure air systems bring rainy, changeable weather to areas in the middle latitudes. They form along the polar front (1), where warm air from the tropics meets cold air from the poles. Warm air flows into bends in the front (2). Finally, a rotating depression is formed with warm light air in the centre, with distinctly colder, heavy air, both behind the warm air and in front of it (3).

Below: This diagram is a section through a depression. It shows the warm air between two areas of cold air. The depression is moving from left to right. The front edge of the warm air at ground level is called the warm front. Here, warm air rises up over the heavier cold air. As it rises, water vapour condenses into clouds and rainstorms occur. The front edge of the cold air is called the cold front. The cold front edges under the warm air as it moves forward. This movement pushes warm air upwards, and so rain clouds also form along the cold front.

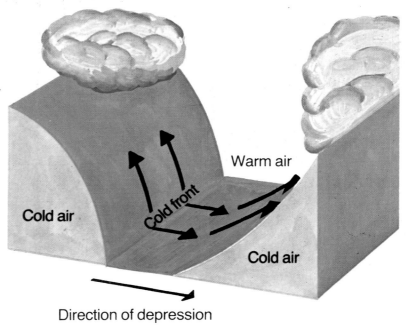

Cold air   Cold front   Warm air   Cold air

Direction of depression

17

Weather stations are now situated in many parts of the world, both on land and on ships at sea. At these stations, meteorologists measure weather conditions.

Some of the instruments used at weather stations are shown on these pages, including cup anemometers to measure wind speeds, vanes to measure wind directions, sunshine recorders, rain gauges, hygrometers (wet and dry bulb thermometers) to determine the relative humidity, and barographs to measure the changing pressure of the air. Some instruments are put in Stevenson screens which shelter them from the Sun, but which allow air to flow through. Other observations made by meteorologists include estimates of the visibility, the amount of the sky covered by cloud, cloud types, and so on. Meteorologists on the thousands of ocean-going ships that serve as weather stations also record special information about the temperature and state of the sea. And a ship's radar can detect rainfall at some distance from it.

Right: Balloons carrying instruments to measure weather conditions in the upper air are released at weather stations. A radio transmitter sends back information.

Sunshine recorders (1) contain a glass sphere that focuses the Sun's rays on to a light-sensitive card, burning a line across it. Rain gauges (2) are sunk into the soil to reduce evaporation. Wind vanes (3) show wind directions, while cup anemometers (4) record wind speeds.

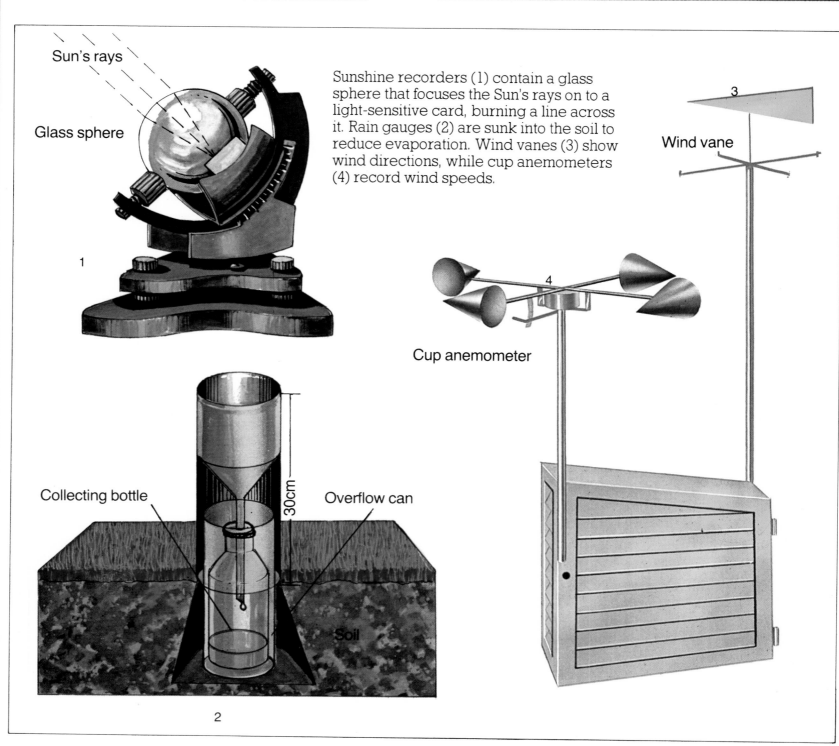

Sun's rays

Glass sphere

1

Collecting bottle   30cm   Overflow can

Soil

2

Wind vane   3

Cup anemometer   4

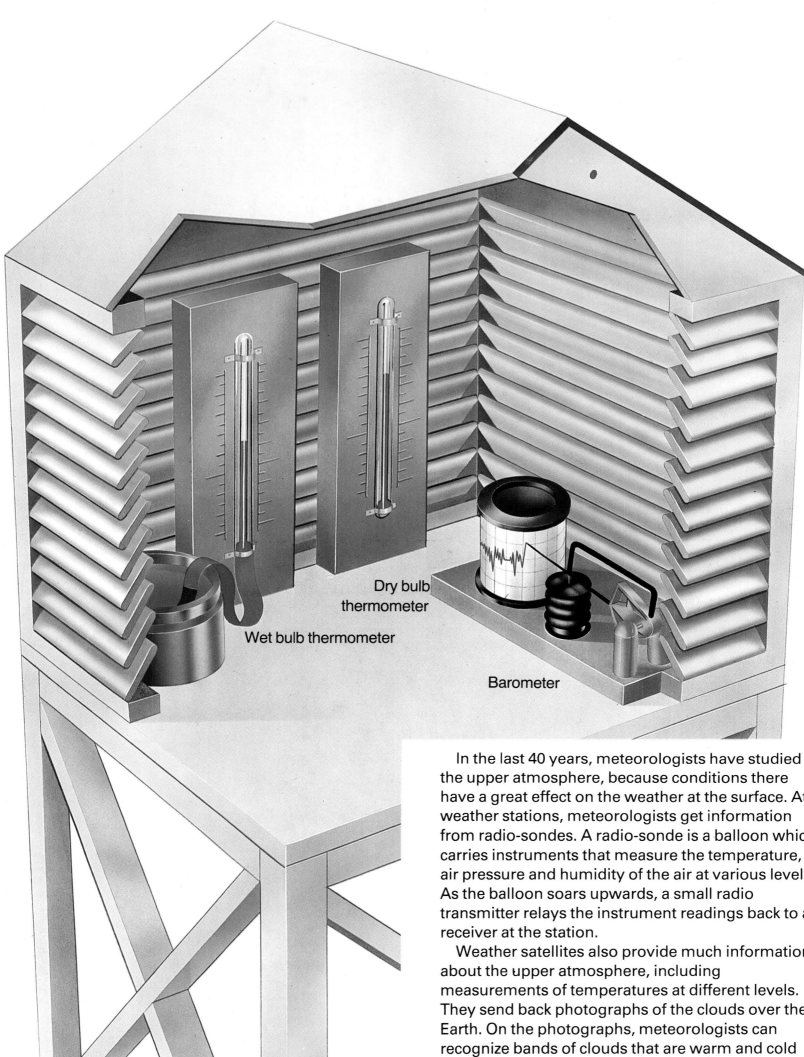

Dry bulb thermometer

Wet bulb thermometer

Barometer

In the last 40 years, meteorologists have studied the upper atmosphere, because conditions there have a great effect on the weather at the surface. At weather stations, meteorologists get information from radio-sondes. A radio-sonde is a balloon which carries instruments that measure the temperature, air pressure and humidity of the air at various levels. As the balloon soars upwards, a small radio transmitter relays the instrument readings back to a receiver at the station.

Weather satellites also provide much information about the upper atmosphere, including measurements of temperatures at different levels. They send back photographs of the clouds over the Earth. On the photographs, meteorologists can recognize bands of clouds that are warm and cold fronts and occlusions. Satellite photographs of a hurricane are shown on pages 20-21.

The information recorded at weather stations is put into code. The code is an international one and can be understood anywhere in the world. The coded information is sent to weather centres, where forecasts are prepared.

The cut-away diagram shows a Stevenson screen. These boxes are used at weather stations to protect instruments from the Sun's rays and radiation from the ground. Air enters freely through the sides, ventilating the box.

Forecasting the Weather

At weather centres, information from weather stations is used to draw weather maps. To speed up this operation, much work is now done by computers. The weather maps show conditions at a particular time. These are called synoptic charts. They give a synopsis, or a summary, of the weather.

To put a lot of information on a map, meteorologists use conventional signs. For example, on weather maps there are lines called isobars, which look like contours. Isobars link places with equal air pressure. The patterns formed by isobars reveal the existence of depressions (lows) and anticyclones (highs). Warm and cold fronts and occlusions are then added.

The meteorologists study the new synoptic chart and compare it with charts showing the weather 6, 12, 18 and 24 hours earlier. They check to see how highs and lows have moved and changed. They also look for any signs of new air systems. From their studies, they work out how they think that the weather will change during the next day.

TRACKING HURRICANES

Storms, called hurricanes, form north and south of the Equator. They contain a warm 'eye' (arrowed), where the air pressure is extremely low. Around it are dark clouds and swirling winds that reach 300 km/h. On average, 11 hurricanes strike the coasts of North America every year. They do much

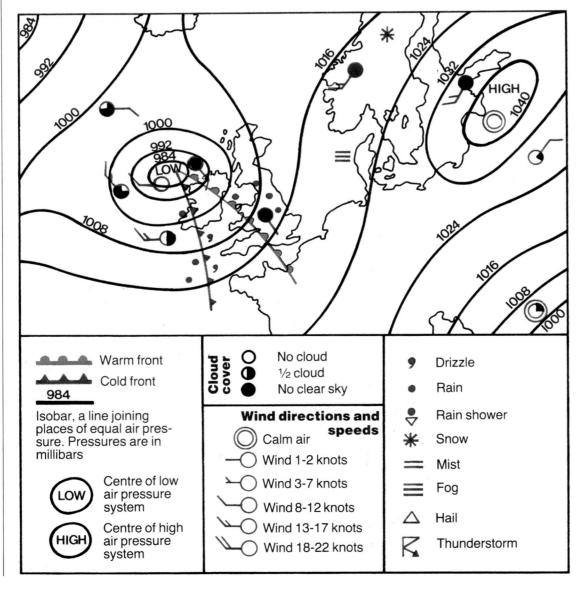

		Cloud cover			
Warm front		○	No cloud	🖋	Drizzle
Cold front		◑	½ cloud	•	Rain
984		●	No clear sky		Rain shower

Isobar, a line joining places of equal air pressure. Pressures are in millibars

Wind directions and speeds

○ Calm air   ※ Snow

LOW — Centre of low air pressure system

○ Wind 1-2 knots   ☰ Mist

HIGH — Centre of high air pressure system

Wind 3-7 knots   ☰ Fog

Wind 8-12 knots   △ Hail

Wind 13-17 knots   ⚡ Thunderstorm

Wind 18-22 knots

Left: Weather maps contain many symbols, depicting air pressure, cloud cover, wind speeds and directions, rain, snow, lightning and air systems called lows (depressions) and highs (anticyclones). 'Synoptic' weather maps give a synopsis or summary of the weather at a particular time. These maps are drawn from information sent to weather centres. 'Prognostic' maps show forecasts of the weather.

Predictions of the future patterns of the weather are put on maps called prognostic (forecast) charts. These maps show the highs, lows and fronts in the positions that the meteorologists expect they will be. From these charts, written forecasts are prepared for various parts of the country.

Weather forecasting is not an exact science. Forecasts must be prepared quickly if they are to be of any use, and they are based on limited information. Also, changes in the atmosphere can occur quickly or in localized areas. For example, meteorologists may forecast thundery showers for a large city on a hot summer day. In the north of the city, the weather may remain fine and people say the forecast is wrong. But the south of the city may have a thunderstorm. Despite their shortcomings, however, weather forecasts are important in our lives.

damage and can cause loss of life. Satellites circling the Earth track these storms. The photographs, above, show the positions of a hurricane a few hours apart. They show how far the eye has moved up the coast (in blue). Study of such photographs enables forecasters to issue storm warnings.

Below: GOES (Geostationary Operational Environmental Satellites) have been used by the United States since the early 1980s. They provide information about weather systems.

Above: Written forecasts are prepared at weather centres from the prognostic charts. They are then issued to television and radio stations. The television announcer explains the forecast to the viewing public. He uses a simplified prognostic chart. Most forecasts are short-range forecasts. This means that they are concerned with the weather over the next 24 hours.

The average weather conditions of a place are called its climate. The most important of these conditions are the average monthly temperatures and the average monthly rainfall. The latitude of a place is a major factor in climate. This is because places near the Equator get much more of the Sun's heat than the polar regions. But the tops of high mountains near the Equator are as cold as polar regions. This is because average temperatures drop by 6 to 7 degrees C for every 1,000 metres as one climbs a mountain.

The terrain also affects the rainfall. Warm, moist winds blowing up mountain slopes lose most of their moisture. But when they blow down the leeward side of mountains, they become warm, drying winds. And places near the sea have a more temperate climate than places in the same latitude in the centre of a land mass.

There are six main climatic regions. *Polar regions* have an average temperature of less than 10 degrees C in the warmest month. *Mountain regions* contain various climatic zones according to height. The *cold temperate regions* of the northern hemisphere are warmer than the polar regions and the average temperature in the warmest month is over 10 degrees C. The cold snowy regions contain huge coniferous forests. The *warm temperate regions* have average temperatures of not more than 18 degrees C in the warmest month. But the average temperature in the coldest month is more than −3 degrees C. The world's *dry climates* have an average yearly rainfall of less than 250 mm. Finally, *tropical rainy regions* have average monthly temperatures of more than 18 degrees C throughout the year.

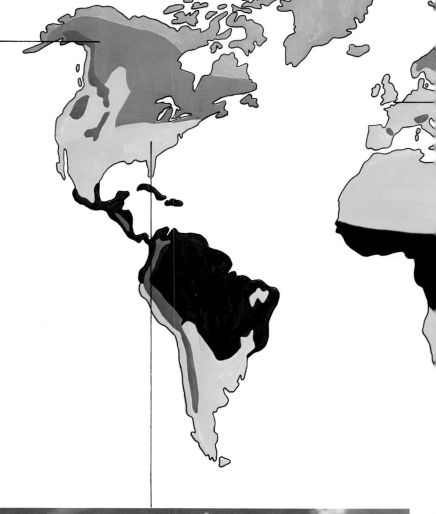

Above: Cottongrass grows in abundance in Alaska in north-western North America during the short, warm summers. Treeless tundra covers much of the interior of Alaska, where the winters are long and bitterly cold.

Below: The fertile plains of Kansas in the United States have a temperate climate. But, because Kansas lies far from the sea, its winters are much colder and its summers hotter than coastal areas in the same latitude.

Left: Finland has a cool temperate climate. Forests of pine, spruce, birch and other trees cover about two-thirds of the land. Coniferous trees survive the cold winters because of their thick barks, shallow roots, needle-like leaves and conical shapes that prevent overloading by snow.

Above: Southern England, with its temperate climate, was once covered by forests of deciduous trees (trees that lose their leaves in winter). Only small patches of these forests remain, including the New Forest in Hampshire, which is beautiful in autumn when the leaves change colour.

Below: Much of Kenya in East Africa has a warm equatorial climate, but it is dry for half of the year. Tropical grassland – savanna – and light forest cover large areas. The savanna supports great herds of grazing animals, such as wildebeest, and various predators, including lions.

Key to map

	Polar
	Mountain
	Cold temperate
	Warm temperate
	Dry
	Tropical rainy

Climate largely determines vegetation. In the tundra regions bordering the snow-covered polar lands, there is a short summer when many small plants grow. But the tundra is too cold for trees. Coniferous trees are adapted to cold temperate climates with warm summers. In the middle latitudes there are several vegetation zones, including grasslands, deciduous (broadleaf) forests and Mediterranean lands. Few plants grow in the hottest deserts, but *xerophytes* (plants adapted to dry climates) grow in semi-deserts.

The animal life of each region is specially adapted to the climate and vegetation. The relationship between animals and the regions in which they live is called 'the balance of nature'. This balance is disturbed when people cut down forests, plough up grasslands or pollute land and water.

Above: This Arctic suslik, which is also called an Arctic ground squirrel, lives near Baker Lake in north-central Canada. Baker Lake is near the Arctic Circle and winters are long and severe. The Arctic suslik eats as much as it can during the short summer and then hibernates for seven months in order to survive the bitterly cold winter.

These Jackass, or Black-footed, penguins gather on Dassin Island, north of Cape Town, to breed. Named because of their braying cry, they live around the coasts of southern Africa. They are fine swimmers and feed mostly on small fish. Their closely-packed feathers and a layer of fat under the skin keep them warm in cold water.

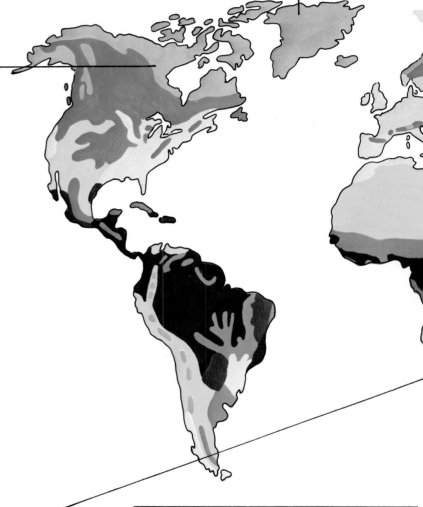

Key to map

- Ice and tundra
- Coniferous forest
- Grasslands
- Desert, semi-desert and scrub
- Temperate forest
- Tropical forest
- Thorn scrub

Left: Polar bears live on the ice floes and in the cold waters of the Arctic Ocean. After leaving their mothers, they lead solitary lives. Some spend part of their time on the northern coasts of Alaska, Canada, Greenland and Russia. Others roam islands in the Arctic Ocean.

Polar bears are well adapted to the climate. Their white coats make them hard to see when they are hunting the seals and young walruses on which they feed. Their dense, greasy fur also keeps them warm, while thick pads of fur on the soles of their feet stop them slipping on the ice. Polar bears have smaller heads, longer necks and more slender bodies than other bears. Their build is adapted for swimming.

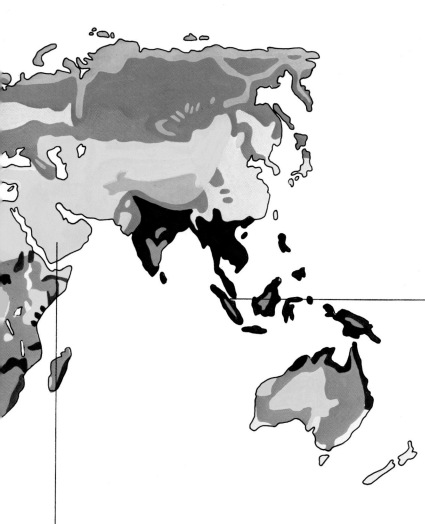

Above: Gibbons are small, lightly built apes with exceptionally long arms. They swing by their arms from branch to branch. Gibbons live in the tropical rain forests of South-East Asia, and on the islands of Borneo, Java and Sumatra. The forest floor is dimly lit because the trees block out sunlight. There is little to eat on the ground, so the gibbons live in the high treetops, where eggs, fruits, insects, leaves and other foods are abundant.

Left: The dromedary or Arabian camel is a fast-running animal. It is used as a beast of burden in the desert lands of south-western Asia and northern Africa. The camel is justly called 'the ship of the desert', because it can travel long distances without drinking. It conserves water because it hardly sweats at all. It gets energy from fat stored in its hump. On long journeys, it can lose water amounting to one-fourth of its body weight. This weight is recovered in 10 minutes, in which time it can gulp down 100 litres of water. The camel's long eyelashes protect its eyes against the Sun and it can shut its narrow nostrils to keep out sand. Its two-toed feet are cushioned to stop them sinking into loose sand.

Equatorial forests grow in low-lying regions between 5 and 10 degrees latitude of the Equator. They have extremely heavy rainfall, much of it being convectional in type, and high temperatures, 25 to 27 degrees C, all the year round. In such conditions, most trees are evergreens, because they can grow throughout the year.

Many valuable species, including ebony, mahogany, rosewood and teak, are found scattered through the forests. Most trees are tall, often more than 30 metres high. They grow to great heights to reach the light, because the forest floor is shaded by the thick foliage above. Because there is little light, the forests usually have little undergrowth. Ground shrubs flourish only where sunlight can penetrate.

The two largest equatorial forests are the Amazon River basin in South America and the Zaire (or Congo) basin in Africa. Much of the Amazon basin, where the forests are called *selvas,* has an average yearly rainfall of 2,000 mm or more. The African forests get less rain, but vast areas have more than 1,300 mm a year.

The hot, humid forests contain many insects, and diseases such as malaria, sleeping sickness and yellow fever are still common. This is one reason why people in the forests often die young. For example, the average life expectancy in Zaire is 47 years, as compared with 74 years in the United States.

Many Indians in the Amazon basin and the pygmies of Africa live off the land. Most farmers live at subsistence level, growing only enough food to feed their families. They often practise shifting farming. This means that they clear a plot in the forest and farm it for a few years. But the heavy rain soon washes out the minerals in the soil that make it fertile. As a result, the farmers soon move on to a new plot. The old farm returns to forest.

Food crops in equatorial forests include cassava and manioc, but there are also large plantations that produce cocoa, coffee, palm-oil, rubber and sugar-cane. Many of these valuable products are exported to other countries. Around the edges of the equatorial forests, the trees thin out into woodland. Beyond are tropical grasslands, called savanna in Africa and llanos or campos in South America. They have a marked dry season.

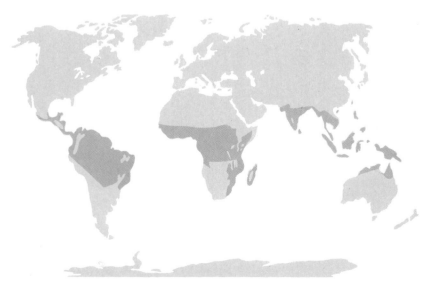

Dense forests cover equatorial regions that have heavy rain and high temperatures throughout the year. Beyond the forests are regions with a dry season. Here the trees thin out into partly wooded tropical grasslands.

Above: East of the high Andes mountains in Peru, the land descends to the upper basin of the mighty Amazon River and its many tributaries. The Amazon basin contains one of the world's greatest equatorial forests. Travelling through the forests is difficult. Most villages and towns are on river banks. The rivers are the main routes for local people who carry forest products in dug-out canoes. Larger boats take out heavy forest products.

Iquitos is the main river port in north-eastern Peru. Large steamers sail up the Amazon River from the Atlantic Ocean as far as Iquitos, a distance of about 3,700 kilometres. The steamers collect produce brought to Iquitos on smaller boats.

Right: These pygmies live in the Ituri Forest of north-eastern Zaire. Pygmies also live in Cameroon, Central African Republic, Congo and Gabon, which all contain, with Zaire, parts of Africa's equatorial forests. The pygmies, who average only 134 to 142 centimetres in height, are hunters. They kill animals with bows and arrows. They live in simple homes made from wooden frames covered by leaves. They also eat berries, roots and insects. Their simple way of life, like that of South American Indians, is now threatened. People from outside are introducing new customs. Some pygmies have already abandoned their traditional life styles and have married into nearby farming communities.

Above: The man is making sago with a traditional bark filter. He lives in a river village in the Sepik river basin of Papua New Guinea. The house is adapted to the equatorial climate. It is built on stilts to keep it dry during floods. Its thick, thatched roof keeps out the heavy rain.

Tropical Monsoon Climates

The word monsoon comes from an Arabic term meaning 'season'. The Arabs use this word for winds in the Arabian Sea that blow for half the year from the south-west and half the year from the north-east. Such wind reversals occur markedly in southern Asia.

In winter, the Asian land mass cools quickly. The cold, dense air forms a large, high-pressure air mass. From this air mass blow the dry north-east trade winds. In March to May, however, the overhead Sun moves northwards, heating the land. This heating causes warm air to rise, creating a marked low pressure air mass.

In early June, the south-east trades are sucked across the Equator into this low pressure air mass, becoming south-west winds. These monsoon winds are warm and moist, having blown across the Indian Ocean. When they reach the land, they bring heavy rain to coastal and upland areas, sometimes causing floods. Cherrapunji, in north-eastern India, holds the world record rainfall for one month – 9,299 mm in July 1861 and also for one year – 26, 461 mm between August 1860 and July 1861. But many inland areas have unreliable rain – heavy in some years, and light or non-existent in others. The south-west winds blow from June to October, continuing in the south until mid-December.

Rain forests similar to equatorial forests grow in the wettest monsoon lands. There are also dry savanna regions, such as the rain shadow area of the Deccan plateau in India. Typical monsoon forests, however, are less dense than equatorial forests and generally contain fewer species. Many of the broad-leaved trees shed their leaves in the dry season, in order to reduce their water loss during the hottest season. Many monsoon regions are thickly populated. Rice is the chief food crop. Cotton, tea and jute are also grown for export.

Right: Lowland or swamp rice is an important food crop that is well adapted to monsoon climates. It probably originated in South-East Asia thousands of years ago. When the monsoon rains arrive, the paddy fields are flooded. Workers transplant young rice plants in the flooded fields. The plants grow in water until they start to ripen. The fields are drained at harvest time. The world's leading rice producers are China, India, Indonesia and Bangladesh.

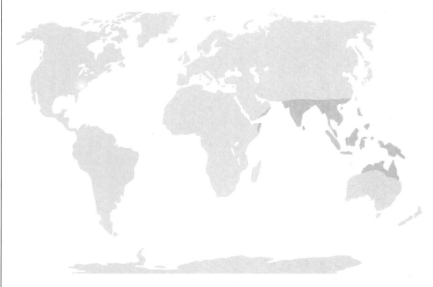

In monsoon regions, the directions of the prevailing winds are reversed between winter and summer. The summer monsoon winds carry much moisture evaporated from the sea. This moisture falls as rain on land areas.

Above: Monsoon lands include some of the world's most thickly populated regions. Even steeply-sloping land must be farmed to produce food. But the rainfall is heavy and it would wash away all the soil on exposed ploughed slopes. To save the soil, farmers build a series of level, step-like terraces down the slopes.

28

Right: This monsoon rain forest is on the Indonesian island of Sulawesi (or Celebes). Such forests are often less dense than equatorial forests that have rain throughout the year. Monsoon forests have a dry winter, when many trees shed their leaves.

Below: Monsoon winds blow in India from June to mid-December. They may bring such heavy rain that rivers overflow their banks. People and animals drown and crops are destroyed. But if the rains fail, droughts cause starvation and death.

The world's hot deserts lie mainly between latitudes 20 degrees and 40 degrees North and South. These are the high air pressure zones of the horse latitudes. Here, the skies are usually clear and cloudless. The air is sinking – the opposite of what happens in the wet equatorial regions. As the air sinks, it becomes warmer and so is able to hold more and more water vapour.

Generally, deserts are places with an average yearly rainfall of less than 250 mm. But, if the evaporation rate is high, places with as much as 500 mm may be barren. Some deserts get no rain. For example, parts of the Atacama desert in northern Chile have had no rain for 400 years. Most deserts have unreliable rainfall. Several years may go by without a drop of rain. Then, a sudden thunderstorm may bring many centimetres in a few hours, causing flooding.

In some areas, plants that have been dormant for years spring to life. They often flower and scatter their seeds within two weeks of sprouting. When this happens in Australia, people travel to see the magnificent sight of the usually parched desert ablaze with colourful plants. The usual plant life in deserts, however, consists of drought-resistant plants, such as the cacti of North America and the tough grasses, scrub and thorn bushes of North Africa and the Middle East. The only places where practically no plants grow are the sand dunes, which cover about one-fifth of the hot deserts.

The richest vegetation is confined to oases, including waterholes and river valleys. The typical plant at Saharan oases is the date palm, but many other fruits and cereals grow in irrigated fields. Deserts can become fertile if water is available. For example, Israeli farmers have set up farms in the barren Negev desert by piping in water from northern Israel.

Oases and river valleys have settled populations, but most deserts are empty except for bands of nomads, who rear camels, goats and sheep. The nomads of the Sahara move around in search of pasture, which they often find in remote mountain areas where the rainfall is a little higher than on the plains.

When hot deserts are irrigated, they can become rich farmland. In Israel, pioneers have turned desert land into farmland. Some water comes from the country's few rivers. Pipes or canals carry it to the fields. Deep below the surface in parts of Israel and other desert regions are layers of porous rocks that are saturated with fresh water.

The beautiful Monument Valley with its rugged 'mesas' (table mountains) and desert scenery straddles the border between Arizona and Utah in the south-western United States. It is the home of the Navajo Indians. The

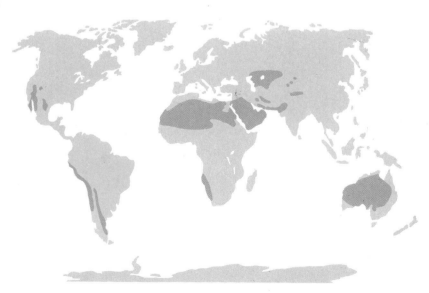

Hot deserts cover about one-fifth of the Earth's land areas. The largest desert is the Sahara in North Africa. Hot deserts lie largely in the horse latitudes, regions of high air pressure from which hot winds blow outwards.

Wells dug down to these rocks tap this underground water, which is drawn to the surface to irrigate the land. Around the wells are green oases, with palm trees and fertile fields of crops.

Some people who live in deserts are farmers at oases. But others are nomads who move around with their herds of animals searching for water and pasture. These nomads in Tunisia live in tents which are light and easy to carry around. The nomads have few possessions. They wear loose, baggy clothes that keep out the sand that is blown about by strong desert winds. In sandstorms, they cover faces with scarves. Only their eyes can be seen.

south-western United States contains several desert regions, including Death Valley, where temperatures in the shade have reached 57°C.

Niger is a large country in North Africa. Most of the country is in the Sahara which contains a few nomadic tribespeople. In the picture, the nomads are watering their animals at a well. Nomads are proud, independent people, with reputations as warriors. Nomadic tribes once fought for control of water-holes.

Several variations exist within the world's warm temperate climates. For example, Britain, northern France and New Zealand have warm summers, cool winters and rain throughout the year. This contrasts with the climate of most nations around the Mediterranean Sea, the California coast in the USA, parts of Chile in South America, the south-western tip of South Africa and parts of southern Australia. These regions have hot summers when little rain falls. This is because they are influenced by the high pressure air systems of the horse latitudes. They share the clear blue skies of the desert regions, although occasional thunderstorms occur. The average temperature in the warmest month is usually above 21 degrees C. In winter, when the climatic zones shift, following the overhead Sun, Mediterranean regions have mild, rainy weather. Average temperatures in the coldest month usually exceed 6 degrees C. The rain comes from depressions.

The plants that thrive in Mediterranean lands are drought-resistant, with deep roots and hard, thick, leathery leaves. Evergreen forests once covered much of the land around the Mediterranean Sea. These forests have been largely cut down. In their place are large tracts of heathland, or shrubby thicket, called 'maquis' and 'garigue'. Maquis consists of tall shrubs and small trees, such as wild olives, myrtles and cork oaks (from which bottle corks are made). Garigue is scattered low shrub. Similar vegetation in the Cape region of South Africa is called 'fynbos', in California 'chaparral', and in Australia 'mallee scrub'.

In the past, agriculture was the main activity in the countries around the Mediterranean Sea. Farms are mostly small, but the land is intensively farmed. Important crops include cereals (mainly barley and wheat, vegetables, olives, grapes and citrus fruits. For example, Italy, Spain and Greece lead the world in producing olive oil, while Italy, France and Spain are the world's chief producers of wine. Today, many people work in industries in the cities, but another major industry has developed in the last 30 years. This is the tourist industry. Tourism has brought prosperity to many previously poor regions.

The Mediterranean climate is named after the climate of most areas bordering the Mediterranean Sea. Similar climates occur in California in the United States, central Chile, southern Africa and in parts of Australia.

Above: The coastal region of central California, in the south-western United States, has a Mediterranean climate. Citrus fruits, including oranges, lemons and grapefruits, flourish in California. Citrus fruits are also grown in all the other Mediterranean regions.

Left: Vineyards are a common sight in countries with a Mediterranean climate. Grapes ripen quickly during the hot, dry summers, such as here on the Portuguese island of Madeira, which is famed for its wine. The terraces on the slopes ensure that every bit of land is cultivated.

Above: Hot, dry and almost continuously sunny summers make coastlands with Mediterranean climates wonderful resorts. In some countries, including Italy, Portugal and Spain, many people work in the tourist industry.

Left: Goats are reared in many Mediterranean lands, such as here in southern Spain. Goats are destructive animals. Left alone, they eat all the plants in an area, rip bark from the trees and tear saplings from the ground. By destroying plants, they expose the soil which is washed away by winter rains. Goats are the main cause of many badly eroded areas in Mediterranean countries.

The polar climates are most developed in Antarctica around the South Pole. Antarctica is larger than either Europe or Oceania, but it has no permanent population. Some scientists spend short periods there studying the climate and the continent's resources. The scientists get all their supplies from the outside world. They live in heated homes under the ice.

The world's lowest air temperature, −88.3 degrees C, was recorded at Vostock Station, between the South Pole and the Shackleton Ice Shelf. The average temperature at Vostok is −55 degrees C (4 degrees C lower than at the South Pole), and ranges from −31 degrees C in January, the warmest month, to −68 degrees C in June, the coldest month. At the poles, because of the Earth's tilt, daylight continues for six months and darkness reigns for the other months.

The air pressure over Antarctica is high, while low pressure air systems encircle the continent. So winds (the polar easterlies) blow outwards from the land to the sea. Snow is the chief form of precipitation, but the total amount of precipitation in Antarctica is less than most deserts get. The snow blown about in blizzards is usually loose snow lifted from the ground rather than new snowfall. But the little snow that does fall piles up year after year to form a huge ice sheet.

The North Pole lies in the centre of the frozen Arctic Ocean. Winters are extremely cold, with average temperatures of −34°C. Like Antarctica, the Arctic has little precipitation. Both places are, therefore, cold deserts. The Arctic Ocean is enclosed by North America, including Greenland (85 per cent of which is covered by ice), Europe and Asia.

The continents contain large areas of tundra. These regions have cold winters and short summers when temperatures rise towards 10°C. In summer, the topsoil melts, but only a few centimetres down the subsoil stays frozen. This subsoil is called permafrost. Trees do not grow in the tundra, but a wide variety of mosses, lichens, flowering plants and shrubs grow in summer. They attract many insects, birds and grazing animals, such as reindeer. The people of the tundra include Eskimos and Lapps.

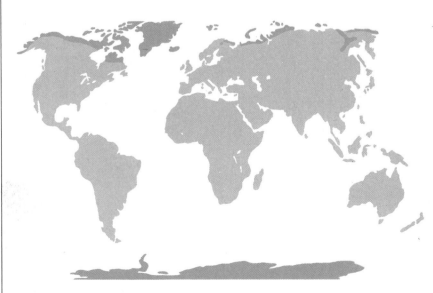

Polar climates occur around the North and South poles. The northern polar regions are surrounded by treeless tundra. The tundra has long, cold winters, but mosses, lichens and some flowering plants grow in the short, warm summers.

Penguins live in the southern hemisphere, mostly in the cold seas around Antarctica. Antarctica is largely covered by the world's biggest ice sheet. Antarctica has no permanent human population.

Right: Icebergs are islands of ice that break away from ice sheets and glaciers and float in the sea. They are a danger to shipping, because eight-ninths of the ice is hidden under the water. Icebergs from Greenland are high and jagged. Icebergs from Antarctica are mostly flat-topped. The largest known iceberg came from Antarctica. It had an area of 31,000 square kilometres.

Above: Eskimos live in the tundra lands that surround the Arctic Ocean. In the past, the lives of these hunting people, including their clothes, homes and means of transport, were largely determined by the harsh climate. But most Eskimos now live in modern homes.

Left: Greenland is a land of snow and ice, lying mainly within the Arctic Circle. It contains the world's second largest ice sheet. The people live in narrow, ice-free coastal areas. January temperatures average −35 degrees C in the north and −7 degrees C in the south.

Going up a mountain, temperatures drop by 6 to 7 degrees C for every 1,000 metres and the air gets thinner. The tops of the highest mountains near the Equator are always snow-capped. The snow-line (the line above which snow does not melt in summer) is at 5,000 to 5,500 metres near the Equator, at 2,700 metres in the Alps, and at sea level near the poles.

Days may be warm on mountains, but temperatures often plummet at night because the thin air cannot retain the heat. Thin air can upset visitors who may get headaches or nosebleeds at 4,000 metres or more.

The vegetation on mountains changes according to height. For example, deciduous forests grow below 760 metres on Mount Washington in New Hampshire in the USA. Above 760 metres is a mixed forest, merging into a coniferous forest at 980 metres. Between 1,220 and 1,520 metres, the forest thins out, merging into treeless tundra. The world's record surface wind speed of 371 kilometres an hour occurred here.

Often the windward sides of mountains have heavy rain and snow, while the leeward sides are dry. In the northern Alps, warm winds blowing down the leeward sides of the mountains are called 'föhn' winds.

Above: The rugged Italian Dolomites reach more than 3,300 metres above sea level. Below a treeless tundra zone are coniferous forests. Deciduous trees grow only in valleys.

Below: Mount Kilimanjaro, which is 5,895 metres above sea level, is Africa's highest peak. It is only about three degrees south of the Equator, but it is always snow-capped.

When climbing a mountain in the tropics, such as Kilimanjaro, you pass through a series of climatic zones. Tropical savanna, with high temperatures all the year round and an average annual rainfall of less than 760mm, extends up to about 1,650 metres. Between 1,650 and 3,000 metres, it is cooler, but the average annual rainfall is about 1,520mm and so there is a belt of rain forest.

At 3,000 metres, the rainfall decreases and a belt of mountain grassland replaces the forests. Between 3,300 and 3,900 metres is a zone of upland moor, where there are many plant species similar to those in temperate regions in the middle latitudes. Above 3,900 metres is alpine tundra, which gives way to permanent snow and ice at about 5,000 metres.

About 120,000 years ago, elephants and lions lived in northern Europe. But 20,000 years ago, ice covered much of the northern hemisphere. These areas were as cold as Antarctica. In AD 984, Norsemen set up a colony on the coast of Greenland, where it was warm enough to grow wheat. By the early 15th century, however, it was so cold that the colony died out.

Scientists have produced many theories to explain why climates change. Recent studies have shown that major volcanic eruptions cause cold weather. Volcanic dust in the stratosphere blocks out sunlight and the Earth is cooled.

But volcanic eruptions cannot explain all climatic changes. Some scientists think that gradual changes in the Earth's path around the Sun and the tilt of its axis cause climatic changes. These changes may have caused the northern latitudes to receive less heat than before and this may have created the Ice Ages.

But why are there coal seams, formed from tropical plants, in Antarctica? The best way to explain this mystery is the theory of continental drift. This says that land masses have moved and are still moving around the face of the Earth.

Stone Age paintings provide clues about the climates of the past. These paintings are on a cave wall at Lascaux, in France. They were painted during the Ice Age, when many animals in the paintings became extinct. Stone Age paintings in the Sahara show that it was a grassland region in the Ice Age.

People can affect climate. For example, farmers have contributed to the southward spread of the Sahara in Africa. Trees have been cut down for firewood, grasslands have been overgrazed by cattle and the land has been intensively farmed. The bare soil has then been worn away by rain and winds.

By studying layers of rocks, geologists can often tell what the climate was like when the rocks were formed. For example, many red sandstones were formed many millions of years ago in ancient deserts, while some limestones, composed largely of ancient coral, were formed in warm, shallow, tropical seas.

This fossil of a giant moss was found in Somerset, in south-western England. This plant once grew in a tropical swamp, where temperatures were far higher than those in Somerset today. Fossils are clues to past climates. They support the theory that land areas have been moved around by continental drift. For example, fossils of ancient reptiles found in Antarctica prove that Antarctica was once much closer to the Equator than it is today.

The last Ice Age started to come to an end about 12,000 years ago. However, it was not until about 10,000 years ago that the climate began to resemble that of the present day. The climate of western Europe has changed many times in the last 10,000 years. Historians have found that there were periods when it was warmer and periods when it was cooler than today. One cool period began in the 15th century and lasted until about 1850. This 'Little Ice Age' reached its height in the 17th century. This picture of the frozen River Thames looking eastward to old London Bridge was painted in 1677. Even in the coldest winters in modern times, the Thames has never frozen over.

Certain features of the weather can cause terrible destruction and loss of life. For example, a storm in the Bay of Bengal in 1970 drove the waves over islands in the Ganges delta of Bangladesh. An estimated one million people were drowned in the floods.

Hurricanes form in the Atlantic Ocean and move west towards North America. Meteorologists give the hurricanes people's names. In 1965 Hurricane Betsy caused $715 million's worth of damage. Hurricane Frederic caused damage valued at $752 million in 1979.

Hurricane-force winds blowing across the open sea create towering waves that may drive ships on to rocks or reefs. The highest recorded wave in the open sea measured 34 metres between its trough and crest. Hurricanes may cause floods along coasts. The flood water sweeps boats inland. The boats are stranded when the waters go down.

Many tropical regions have an average yearly rainfall that is sufficient for crops to grow. But the rainfall is often unreliable. In some years, the total rainfall may be much above average, but wet years are often followed by years of drought. Crops shrivel up in the parched soil. Cattle die through lack of pasture, and people starve.

Tornadoes are small but intense storms, with extremely low air pressures. About 500 to 600 tornadoes are reported in the United States every year. In March 1925, a tornado in the south-central states of the USA caused the deaths of 689 people.

Famines caused by droughts can be responsible for the deaths of millions of people and animals, especially in densely populated areas, such as India and China. Another spectacular weather feature is lightning. One bolt of lightning killed 21 people in Zimbabwe in 1975.

Tornadoes are very destructive storms. They start when a narrow column of air sinks down from a cumulonimbus cloud. Warm air rises and spirals around this column.

Tornadoes measure less than one-half of a kilometre across, but winds in them reach 650 km/h. Tornadoes leave a trail of destruction as they move across country.

Floods occur in several ways. Coastal floods are often caused by storm waves. Inland floods may occur when dams are breached or when rivers overflow their banks.

Rivers are sometimes swollen by heavy rain or by melt water created when unusually warm weather in spring melts snow near the sources of the rivers.

Since the Industrial Revolution in Britain, which began in the late 18th century, factories have poured smoke and gases into the air. Some industrial cities have suffered unpleasant smog, a mixture of smoke and fog. Also sulphur dioxide mixed with rainwater has eaten away many metals and stonework. Some cities, including Los Angeles in the USA, are often covered by a yellow haze. This kind of smog is caused by vehicle exhaust gases which contain carbon monoxide, nitrogen oxide and hydrocarbons. Sunlight reacts with these substances to form *photochemical smog,* which makes peoples' eyes water. To reduce air pollution, some countries make people use smokeless fuels in industrial regions. And, since 1968, the US government has made manufacturers reduce the pollutants given off in vehicle exhausts.

Since the start of the Industrial Revolution, the amount of carbon dioxide in the atmosphere has perhaps increased by between 20 and 25 per cent. Carbon dioxide is released into the air by the burning of coal, oil and gas. Some scientists think that an increase of carbon dioxide will, before long, start to warm the Earth. Ice sheets will then start to melt. The sea level will rise and great cities will vanish under the waves.

Other air pollution caused by man includes radioactive fallout from hydrogen bomb explosions and, possibly in the near future, pollution by spacecraft. Some scientists fear that, if space travel increases, rocket motor exhaust gases might upset the delicate ozone layer in the stratosphere. Were this to happen, we would be roasted by the Sun's ultraviolet rays.

Unpleasant smog pollutes the air over the city of São Paulo, Brazil, which is South America's greatest industrial centre. Smog is a word made up of parts of two other words, smoke and fog. Fog is a mass of tiny water droplets in the air. But smog is a fog mixed with tiny particles of smoke and dust and the gas sulphur dioxide. These substances are released by the burning of coal in homes and factories.

Factory smoke and gases may form smog. Sometimes, smog lasts for several days, because the air near the ground is chilled so that it is colder and denser than the warmer air above. Because of this, the dirty air cannot rise

After cleaning

Britain's capital city of London once suffered from severe smogs. However, in 1956, the government passed a Clean Air Act. People then had to use smokeless fuels both in homes and factories. This law greatly reduced pollution and London no longer suffers from smog, although car exhaust gases still pollute the air. In the past, smog-blackened buildings, and stone and metals were worn away by rainwater which was turned into sulphuric acid by mixing with chemicals in the air. In recent years, London has been gradually cleaned. The photograph, top, shows the famous statue of Lord Nelson in Trafalgar Square being cleaned. The second photograph shows how its original colour has been restored.

upward and disperse. Severe smog reduces visibility and can cause chest diseases. In December 1952, a smog that could not escape because of a temperature inversion killed an estimated 4,000 people in London.

The climate has a tremendous influence on plant, animal and human life. It affects the clothes we wear, the food we eat, the homes we live in, our holidays and recreation, the diseases that make us ill, and so on. Some scientists think that people are most efficient in temperate climates.

In fact, scientists have claimed that people are most energetic when temperatures average 18 degrees C and relative humidities are 70 to 80 per cent, providing that there are frequent changes in the weather to keep people alert.

Of all human activities, farming is most at the mercy of the weather. Arable (crop) farming is confined to about 10 per cent of the world's land areas, while pasture covers about 20 per cent. The rest of the world is unsuitable for agriculture, unless special conditions are created, for example by using greenhouses.

The design of houses around the world varies according to the climate. In parts of the interior of Iran, in the Middle East, July temperatures soar to 55°C. In such places, the houses have no windows and their walls are made especially thick to keep out the Sun's burning heat. Tall wind towers are attached to some of the buildings. These towers contain holes near the top. The holes direct the slightest of breezes downwards into the house. This draught of air helps to ventilate the rooms and keep them cool. A more expensive, but much more efficient way of keeping people cool in hot climates is the use of modern air-conditioning systems.

Fog is usually less than 300 metres deep. But it can be so dense that it is a great hazard to transport. Many terrible accidents occur on motorways when cars, which are moving too fast, crash into each other in patches of fog. Fog is a problem in many countries, such as Britain where the city of Birmingham, centre of a motorway network, has an average of 59 foggy days a year. This is nearly one day out of every six. Weather forecasts which can be heard on car radios include fog warnings. Vast amounts of money are also spent on lighting and fog-warning equipment in order to reduce accidents.

Fog is also a danger to ships and aircraft, although the use of radar has greatly cut down the number of accidents at sea and at airports. Sea fog is usually caused when warm air blows over a cold stretch of water and the water vapour in the air condenses. For example, sea fogs are common off Newfoundland in Canada. They occur when warm air over the Gulf Stream passes over the cold Labrador Current.

These heated greenhouses in the mild, sunny Channel Islands show how people can control the climate. The farmers here grow crops like tomatoes out of season. At such times, the demand and the prices for such crops are high. However, farming, perhaps more than any other human activity, is controlled by climate. Each plant requires a particular kind of climate in which to grow. For example, bananas and pineapples are not grown in northern and central Europe because the climate is too cold. But even tropical fruits could be grown in greenhouses if there was enough demand for them.

Most crops grow in the open air. As a result, farmers rely on weather forecasts. They need to know whether damaging frosts or hailstorms are likely to occur. With advance warning, they take steps to protect their plants. For example, some farmers use braziers to warm the air and so combat the effects of currents of cold air. In some countries, special local forecasts are available for farmers.

The weather affects both the players and spectators of sports. Sudden downpours of rain can interrupt golf tournaments, such as here when the British golfer Peter Oosterhuis and the crowd get drenched as they wait for the rain to stop. Rainy weather can lead to a great loss of money in several sports, such as cricket and lawn tennis, although tennis can be played in covered courts. And horse racing, soccer and rugby football may be cancelled in winter when frost makes the ground so hard that it is dangerous to use. In Europe, undersoil heating and warm-air plastic covers have been used by some clubs to combat frost. Machines for drying wet grounds are being developed for many sports and, in North America, football and baseball are often played on artificial turf. But such developments are expensive. The weather also affects holidays. The weather in the middle latitudes is so changeable that many holiday-makers travel long distances to obtain a sunny, rain-free few weeks.

In rich, developed countries, the effects of climate can be reduced. For example, many roads in poor countries are dirt tracks. After heavy rains, these tracks become muddy and impassable. But in rich countries, roads are surfaced and are kept open except in the worst weather. The same applies to housing. Those who can afford central heating and air conditioning now live comfortably anywhere in the world.

The American writer Mark Twain once said of the weather: 'Everybody talks about it, but nobody ever does anything about it'. This is no longer true. In the last 40 years, rain has been successfully created by 'seeding' clouds (*see page 16*). In many countries, explosive rockets are fired into rain clouds to shatter hailstones before they destroy the crops below. Scientists are also studying ways of harnessing elements of the weather, including the Sun's heat and winds, to produce electric power. This work is important, because oil and natural gas reserves are running down.

The success of the human race on Earth has been based on the ability of people to adapt and change their environment. For example, deserts have been made fertile. And biologists have produced special varieties of crops that grow well in climates where traditional varieties do not survive. Scientists have also searched for ways of changing climates so that more land areas could be farmed. They have suggested that a dam be built across the Bering Strait, between Asia and North America. If cold water was pumped out of the Arctic Ocean through this dam, more warm water would enter from the North Atlantic and make the Arctic regions milder.

But such changes might have effects that scientists cannot foresee. Many dangers exist if we disturb the delicate balance of nature. Before we interfere with climates, we must have a better understanding of the science of meteorology.

Kufra, in the Libyan desert (part of the Sahara) was once a tiny oasis. In 1967 large amounts of water were found underground. Wells now tap this water, which irrigates much farmland which was formerly a dry wasteland.

Anabatic wind A wind that blows up a valley or mountain slope. It occurs when the Sun heats mountain slopes, causing air to rise. Cool air from below then flows upwards to replace the rising air.

Anticyclone A high pressure air system, associated with settled weather. Permanent anticyclones are found over the horse latitudes.

Barometer An instrument to measure air pressure. There are several types, including mercury barometers and aneroid barometers.

Blizzard A fast wind blowing loose snow and sometimes ice crystals.

Bora A cold, north-easterly wind that blows in winter from central Europe and the Balkans (high pressure areas) to the eastern coast of the Adriatic Sea and northern Italy.

Chinook A warm, föhn-like wind blowing down the eastern side of the Rocky Mountains in North America.

Convection current A current in the air (or a fluid) caused when heating from below expands the air, making it rise. Cool air flows in to replace it.

Cyclone A low pressure air system, commonly called a depression. A tropical cyclone is a hurricane.

Depression See Cyclone.

Dew point The temperature at which air is saturated with water.

Dust devil A small whirlwind, caused by convection currents, carrying dust up to 600-900 metres over deserts.

Duststorm Large areas of wind-blown dust that reduce visibility over deserts and up to 3,000 metres in the air. They are a danger to aircraft.

Föhn wind A warm wind blowing down the northern slopes of the Alps. It occurs when there are depressions to the north of the Alps.

Front A line separating areas of cold and warm air.

Harmattan A hot, dry, dusty wind from the Sahara. It is felt along the West African coasts and often damages crops.

Hydrological cycle Another name for the water cycle.

Hygrometer An instrument to measure relative humidity, such as a wet and dry bulb thermometer.

Insolation The energy received by the Earth from the Sun.

Isobar A line on a map linking places with an equal air pressure.

Isohyet A line on a map linking places with the same rainfall.

Isotherm A line on a map linking places with the same temperature.

Jet stream A strong westerly wind that blows near the tropopause in middle latitudes.

Katabatic wind A cold wind blowing down mountain and valley slopes, often at night when higher slopes cool quicker than sheltered valleys.

Khamsin A hot, dry, dusty wind blowing from the Sahara into Egypt.

Land and sea breezes Local winds on coasts. By day, the land heats faster than the sea, so cool air from the sea blows on to the land. By night, the land cools faster than the sea, so breezes blow from the land to the sea.

Lightning A huge spark (a discharge of electricity) in thunderstorms. The heat generated by lightning makes the air expand quickly, causing thunder.

Millibar A unit of atmospheric pressure; 1,000 millibars equals one bar (or 750.1 mm of mercury).

Mistral A cold, north-westerly wind blowing from the centre of Europe to the shores of the north-western Mediterranean Sea, usually in winter.

Nor-wester A hot, dry wind blowing down mountain slopes in South Island, New Zealand.

Permafrost Ground that is permanently frozen, like the subsoil in tundra regions.

Precipitation Deposits of water, either liquid or solid, that come from the atmosphere, including rain, snow, sleet, hail, dew and frost.

Rainbow An arc of coloured light caused by the reflection and refraction of the Sun's rays by drops of water.

Samoon A hot, dry wind blowing down mountain slopes in Iran.

Simoom A hot, dry, dusty wind in the Sahara and in Arabia, chiefly in spring and summer.

Sirocco A hot, dry, dusty wind blowing from the Sahara to Sicily and southern Italy.

Thermometer An instrument to measure temperatures, usually consisting of mercury or alcohol in a glass tube with a bulb at the bottom.

Thunder See Lightning.

Waterspout A storm similar to a tornado but over the sea.

Whirlwind A small column of rotating air around a low air pressure core.

Willy-Willy The name for a tropical cyclone in north-western Australia.

Zonda A hot, humid wind blowing from the north into Argentina and Uruguay, *or a föhn*-type wind blowing down the eastern slopes of the Andes.

Below: The Tuaregs of the Sahara cover their faces during choking duststorms. Duststorms are caused by strong winds.